Fact Finders™

Biographies

Christopher
COLUMBUS

by Mervyn D. Kaufman

Consultant:

John P. Boubel, Ph.D.
History Professor, Bethany Lutheran College
Mankato, Minnesota

Capstone
press

Mankato, Minnesota

Fact Finders is published by Capstone Press
151 Good Counsel Drive, P.O. Box 669, Mankato, Minnesota 56002
www.capstonepress.com

Library of Congress Cataloging-in-Publication Data
Kaufman, Mervyn D.
    Christopher Columbus / by Mervyn D. Kaufman.
    p. cm.—(Fact finders. Biographies)
    Summary: An introduction to the life of fifteenth-century Italian explorer Christopher
Columbus, whose travels helped map our modern world.
    Includes bibliographical references and index.
    ISBN 0-7368-2486-3 (hardcover)
    1. Columbus, Christopher—Juvenile literature. 2. Explorers—America—Biography—
Juvenile literature. 3. Explorers—Spain—Biography—Juvenile literature. 4. America—
Discovery and exploration—Spanish—Juvenile literature. [1. Columbus, Christopher.
2. Explorers. 3. America—Discovery and exploration—Spanish.] I. Title. II. Series.
E111.K19 2004
970.01′5′092—dc22   2003015254

Editorial Credits
Roberta Schmidt, editor; Juliette Peters, series designer and illustrator; Linda Clavel and
    Heather Kindseth, illustrators; Deirdre Barton, photo researcher; Eric Kudalis,
    product planning editor

Photo Credits
Art Resource/Albert Bierstadt (1830–1902) The Newark Museum, 20–21; Giraudon, 1;
    Peter Frederick Rothermel (1817–1895) Smithsonian American Art Museum,
    Washington D.C., 15
Corbis/Gianni Dagli, 12; Historical Picture Archive, 22; Swim Ink, 10–11
Getty Images/Hulton Archive, cover, 4–5, 8, 18–19; Eugene Deveria-Roger Viollet, 24–25
Keystone, 16–17
Mary Evans Picture Library, 7
North Wind Picture Archives, 9, 13, 14
Stock Montage Inc., 23

1 2 3 4 5 6 09 08 07 06 05 04

Table of Contents

Chapter 1

A Great Discovery

"Land! Land!"

A man was yelling to the other sailors. In the moonlight, he could see the white sand of a beach. Their long **voyage** was over.

It was October 12, 1492. At daybreak, some of the men got into small rowboats and went to shore. The sailors watched as their captain knelt on the beach and said a prayer.

All of the men were thankful for reaching solid ground. They had not seen land in more than a month. At one point, the sailors had almost thrown their captain overboard so they could go back home.

The sailors were happy to see land after many weeks at sea.

The captain finished his prayer and stood up. He was a tall man with light eyes. His name was Christopher Columbus.

Chapter 2

A Beginning in Genoa

Christopher Columbus was born in 1451. He grew up in Genoa. This large city rested on the edge of the Mediterranean Sea. Genoa later became part of Italy. Goods from all over the world came through Genoa.

As a child, Columbus helped his father, Domenico. They wove wool. Columbus' mother, Susanna, also helped weave wool.

Columbus often went to the **docks** to watch the ships. He listened to the traders and sailors talk about their adventures. He knew he wanted to be a sailor when he grew up.

Columbus lived in a part of Genoa called Porta Sovrano.

Columbus Goes to Sea

Columbus went to sea when he was a young man. For five years, he worked on ships in the Mediterranean Sea. He learned about sailing.

In 1476, Columbus was on a ship going to northern Europe. As they passed the coast of Portugal, the ship was attacked by pirates.

Columbus was wounded and thrown into the water. He clung to an oar and swam 6 miles (10 kilometers) to the Portuguese shore.

Columbus spent many years on ships. He learned about sailing.
◄

Columbus stayed in Portugal for several years. He married a Portuguese woman and had a son. He also taught himself to read and write Spanish and Latin.

Over the next few years, Columbus planned a new adventure. He wanted to reach Asia by sailing west.

Columbus studied many
▼ maps to plan his voyage.

Chapter 3

Eastern Lands

In the late 1400s, Europeans were looking for new ways to reach far eastern lands. These lands included Japan, China, India, and the Indies. The Indies are the islands of southeastern Asia. These lands had silk and spices not found in Europe. Europeans especially wanted these items.

Trading with Asia was hard. People who lived between western Europe and southeastern Asia controlled the trade. They made Europeans pay high prices for goods.

Europeans decided to try to trade directly with Asia. But first they had to find a new way to reach Asia. Some people started to search for a way to sail around Africa.

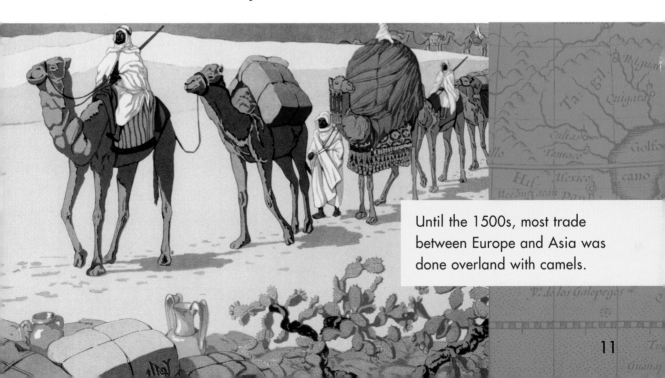

Until the 1500s, most trade between Europe and Asia was done overland with camels.

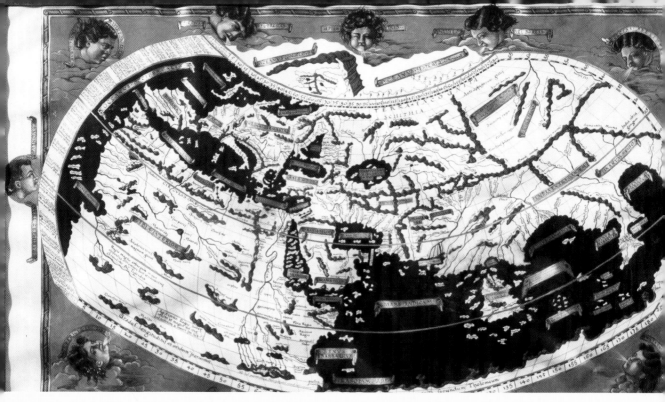

▲ This 1400s world map shows that Europeans did not know about the Americas.

Columbus believed he could find a shorter route to Asia. He would sail west. Since the world was round, he knew he would eventually reach the Indies in the East. He only had to cross the Atlantic Ocean between Europe and Asia. At that time, people called the Atlantic Ocean the Ocean Sea.

FACT!

In the 1400s, Europeans did not know much about the world. They thought there was only one ocean. They also did not know there were more lands than Europe, Africa, and Asia.

Columbus wanted to bring the riches of the Indies back to Europe. He read about those riches in Marco Polo's book. Polo traveled to Asia almost 200 years before Columbus was born. Polo wrote about the gold and other riches he saw there.

Columbus had another reason to reach the Indies. He wanted to teach the Christian religion to the people there.

Marco Polo explored Asia from ▼ 1271 to 1295.

13

▲ Columbus and his son traveled to Spain in 1485.

Asking for Help

Columbus knew he would need help to make the voyage. He needed money, ships, supplies, and a good crew. He decided to ask the kings and queens of Europe for help.

For more than seven years, Columbus asked for help. He started with King John of Portugal. King John said no.

In 1485, Columbus' wife died, and Columbus and his son went to Spain. But Columbus had to wait to talk to King Ferdinand and Queen Isabella. Spain was fighting a war.

In 1488, Columbus went back to Portugal. But that year, a Portuguese man named Bartolomeu Dias sailed to the southern tip of Africa. Dias said a ship could sail that way and reach India. King John did not need another way to Asia. Columbus went back to Spain.

In 1492, Spain won its war. The country had money to spare. Queen Isabella agreed to help Columbus.

Columbus convinced Queen Isabella ▼ to help him.

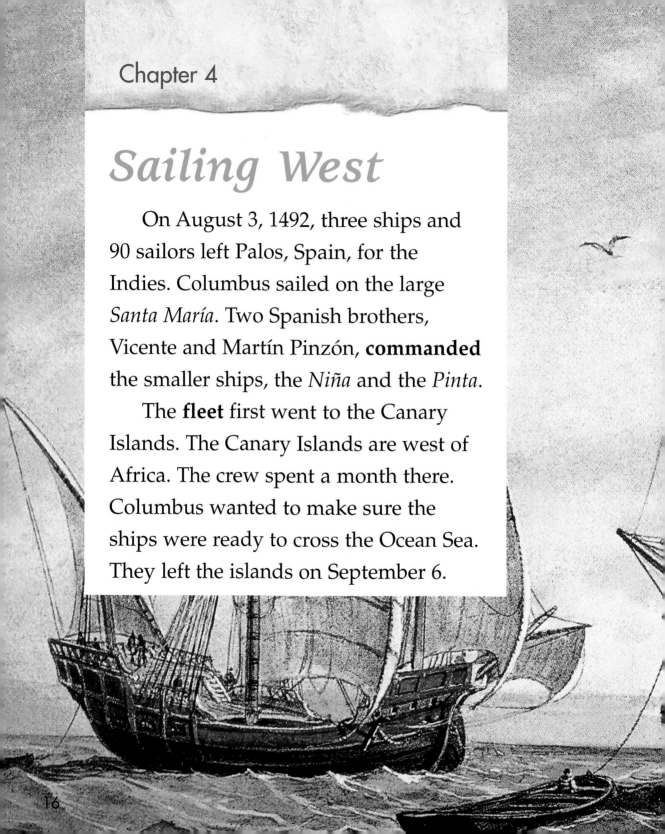

Chapter 4

Sailing West

On August 3, 1492, three ships and 90 sailors left Palos, Spain, for the Indies. Columbus sailed on the large *Santa María*. Two Spanish brothers, Vicente and Martín Pinzón, **commanded** the smaller ships, the *Niña* and the *Pinta*.

The **fleet** first went to the Canary Islands. The Canary Islands are west of Africa. The crew spent a month there. Columbus wanted to make sure the ships were ready to cross the Ocean Sea. They left the islands on September 6.

Columbus' ships were called the *Niña*, the *Pinta*, and the *Santa María*.

17

The ships sailed west. Some days, no wind blew. On these days, the ships barely moved across the calm water. At one point, thick yellow and green seaweed filled the water. Some of the sailors became afraid. They had heard stories about sea monsters in the Ocean Sea. But the ships sailed on.

Columbus kept a journal about the trip. He wrote how far they traveled each day. He never showed this journal to the men. He knew the sailors would be even more afraid if they knew they had traveled so far.

Many sailors became angry with Columbus. They wanted to go back to Spain.

After a month at sea, the sailors became worried. None of them had ever sailed so long without seeing land. Some of them wanted to throw Columbus overboard. They wanted to turn around and go home.

On October 10, 1492, Columbus finally agreed with the men. He said that if they did not see land within three days, they would turn around and go home. Two days later, a sailor on the *Pinta* yelled, "Land! Land!"

F A C T !

Young boys helped on the ships. Some boys cooked. They made one hot meal for the sailors each day.

Chapter 5

The "Indies"

After Columbus reached shore and said a prayer, he **claimed** the land for Spain. He then named the island San Salvador.

Columbus and the sailors saw people watching them. Columbus was so sure he had reached the Indies that he called these people "Indians." The Indians were friendly. They gave Columbus parrots, cotton thread, and other gifts.

FACT!

No one is sure on which island Columbus landed. Most people believe he landed on Watling's Island, now called San Salvador.

On October 12, 1492, Columbus landed on the island he named San Salvador.

Over the next few weeks, Columbus **explored** many islands. Almost all of the people there were kind and helpful. They gave Columbus food and gold for European goods. Columbus wrote about these Indians. They were willing to do anything he asked. He noted that they would make good slaves.

Columbus traded with
▼ the Indians.

22

On Christmas Eve, the *Santa María* sailed too close to an island. It was damaged on a large rock. The Indians helped the sailors get everything off the ship before it sank. The sailors used wood from the ship to make a fort on the island.

Columbus named the island *La Isla Española*. It became known as Hispaniola. Today, the countries of Haiti and the Dominican Republic make up this island.

On January 4, 1493, Columbus started the long trip back to Spain. He had many things to show the king and queen.

▲ The *Santa María* was destroyed on December 24, 1492.

Chapter 6

A Hero Returns

On March 15, 1493, the *Niña* and *Pinta* sailed into the port of Palos, Spain. The people of Spain welcomed Columbus as a hero. They stared at everything Columbus had brought back, from the parrots to the Indians.

Columbus went to King Ferdinand and Queen Isabella. He told them many stories about his adventure. He told them that he had reached the Indies. He was sure he would find the gold and riches there on his next trip.

FACT!

Spain gave Columbus titles of honor. He was called Admiral of the Ocean Sea and Viceroy and Governor of the Islands.

Columbus brought Indians and gifts to King Ferdinand and Queen Isabella.

Lasting Impact

Over the next 11 years, Columbus crossed the Ocean Sea three more times. He explored many more islands. He found many more Indians. He did not find much gold.

Columbus died in Valladolid, Spain, on May 20, 1506. He always believed he had found a new route to the Indies. After Columbus, many people crossed the Ocean Sea. They realized that the islands were not part of Asia.

Columbus had led Europeans to a land unknown to them. Although he never saw the mainland of North America, Christopher Columbus would be remembered as the man who discovered America for the Europeans.

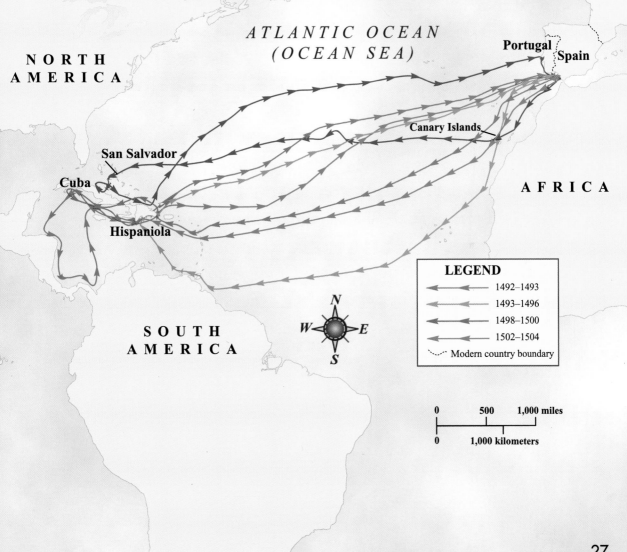

The Voyages of Christopher Columbus, 1492–1504

**ATLANTIC OCEAN
(OCEAN SEA)**

**NORTH
AMERICA**

Portugal **Spain**

San Salvador

Canary Islands

Cuba

AFRICA

Hispaniola

**SOUTH
AMERICA**

N
W · E
S

LEGEND

←	1492–1493
←	1493–1496
←	1498–1500
←	1502–1504
⋯	Modern country boundary

0   500   1,000 miles

0   1,000 kilometers

Fast Facts

- Columbus grew up in Genoa. He wanted to be a sailor.

- In 1492, the queen of Spain agreed to help Columbus sail west to reach Asia.

- Columbus left Spain on August 3, 1492. He had three ships called the *Niña*, the *Pinta*, and the *Santa María*.

- Columbus reached San Salvador on October 12, 1492.

- Columbus believed he had reached the Indies of southeastern Asia. He called the people he met "Indians."

- Columbus is remembered as the man who discovered the Americas for the Europeans.

Time Line

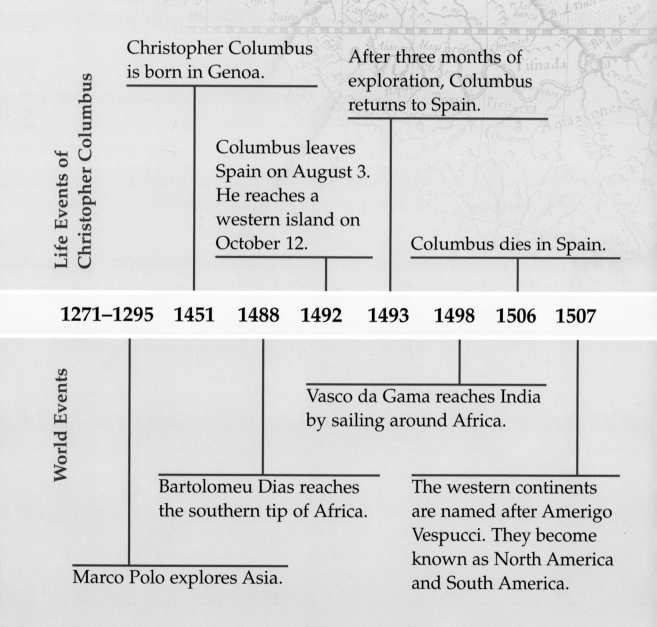

Life Events of Christopher Columbus

Christopher Columbus is born in Genoa.

Columbus leaves Spain on August 3. He reaches a western island on October 12.

After three months of exploration, Columbus returns to Spain.

Columbus dies in Spain.

1271–1295 1451 1488 1492 1493 1498 1506 1507

World Events

Marco Polo explores Asia.

Bartolomeu Dias reaches the southern tip of Africa.

Vasco da Gama reaches India by sailing around Africa.

The western continents are named after Amerigo Vespucci. They become known as North America and South America.

Glossary

claim (KLAYM)—to say that something belongs to you or that you have a right to have it

command (kuh-MAND)—to have control over something

dock (DOK)—a place where ships load and unload cargo

explore (ek-SPLOR)—to travel to find out what a place is like

fleet (FLEET)—a group of ships that sail together

voyage (VOI-ij)—a long journey

Internet Sites

FactHound offers a safe, fun way to find Internet sites related to this book. All of the sites on FactHound have been researched by our staff.

Here's how:
1. Visit *www.facthound.com*
2. Type in this special code **0736824863** for age-appropriate sites. Or enter a search word related to this book for a more general search.
3. Click on the **Fetch It** button.

FactHound will fetch the best sites for you!

Read More

Alter, Judy. *Christopher Columbus: Explorer.* Our People. Chanhassen, Minn.: Child's World, 2003.

Kline, Trish. *Christopher Columbus.* Discover the Life of an Explorer. Vero Beach, Fla.: Rourke, 2002.

Larkin, Tanya. *Christopher Columbus.* Famous Explorers. New York: PowerKids Press, 2001.

Reid, Struan. *Christopher Columbus.* Groundbreakers. Chicago: Heinemann Library, 2002.

Index